Poetry Shack 3

compiled by
David Orme and James Sale

Longman

The Pinball Manifesto

ALLAN KORNBLUM

How to use this book

We hope you will enjoy reading and listening to the poems in this book, and that you will enjoy the activities that go with them.

Reading the poems
Don't rush on to the activities until you have spent time enjoying the poems!

You should:

- listen to them read to you
- read them silently a number of times
- talk about them in class or small groups.

Poems use language in a very special way and your discussion will help you understand anything you find puzzling. Remember though, that no poem can be completely 'worked out' like a crossword puzzle. In good poems, there is always something new to be found and thought about every time you read them.

The activities
Many of the activities are designed to help you in your understanding of the poems in this book and of other poems you might read. Other activities suggest ideas for your own writing, for the best way to understand how writers work is to try it yourself! A few of the poems in the collection were written by poets still at school, and we have marked these with * in the Contents list.

David Orme and James Sale

Contents

About Us

1 Womankind

Eulogy for the Era

Beginning with:
Mankind, Man made, the Common Man, Man and his world,
Neanderthal Man, the best Man for the job, when Man
invented the wheel, the Sun God, Man's achievements. Man's
basic needs. The history of black Man in America. One small
step for Man. A giant step for Mankind. Man, like other
mammals, breast feeds his young:

> pressman, repairman, craftsman, chairman, conductor,
> railroad man, switchman,
> maid

> salesman, newsboy, fireman, foreman
> master, policeman, watchman
> laundress

> clergyman, delivery man, fisherman,
> lineman, jack-of-all-trades,
> wife

We hold these truths to be self-evident: That all men are
created equal...the farmer and his wife, the lawyer and his
child, the poet and his wife, the teacher and her class.

The Greeks mistreated their wives. Columbus discovered
America. The settlers moved west with their wives and their
cattle. A man makes art because he has to. Doctor Jones and his
pert wife Jane. Marie Curie, the beautiful chemist, Elinor
Wylie, the fiery red head, Amy Lowell, the queer duck!

Masculine: resembling man, having vigour and strength
Feminine: resembling woman, showing delicacy and
weakness.

I'll have my girl make your reservations. Union members and
their wives are invited. You drive like an old woman. The
ladies chatted about the draft. Sally's husband lets her work
part-time. Children look to their fathers for strength and
courage. In the delicate recesses of the female mind is the seed
of love.

We look to:
Wise men to free us from superstition and from the old wives'
tales of our forefathers. The litany repeats. Words and the
people they create move in pilgrimage across the earth, a
woman, whose spine is a footprint.

SUSAN BRIGHT

The various words and phrases in this poem make Susan Bright
angry. Choose two each and tell the class why you think they do so.

Use your dictionary to look up any words you do not understand in
the poem; the words in the title, for example.

Write your own definition of 'masculine' and 'feminine', then see
how your own dictionary defines these words.

Ballad of the Dreamy Girl

A pigtail dangled down my back,
I was just sixteen years.
One day my mother came and flicked
a duster round my ears.

'Don't sit there writing poetry,
go dust your room instead!
With all this nonsense you won't earn
the butter on your bread!'

She often scolded me, but I
stepped lightly as a bird
and went on dreaming through the day
as if I had not heard.

What could I say? My mother
would never understand.
So I wrote only secretly,
the duster in my hand.

When finally I learned to cook,
I often heard her tell:
'To keep your future husband sweet,
you'll have to feed him well!'

'And how do men keep women sweet?'
She gave me no reply
but went on cooking, and I saw
her shake her head and sigh.

EDITH ROSEVEARE

What do you think makes a 'good housewife'?
Why does the Dreamy Girl's mother give no reply to the question
she is asked? What do you think the answer is?

Thirteen

She's learnt to spit
through her teeth.
Spectacular.
Stands on the front step
spraying a rose bush.

Craftier than a camel
she licks her lips
with a huge pink tongue,
sucks in her cheeks,
does Donald Duck –

leaps upstairs to change
– she's resewn the split
in her shirt so often
it looks like spiderwebs –
swoops down in purple jeans.

Last month she made a trifle.
It slopped home
like scrambled egg
(she'd used it to hit
some lad over the head).

Her diet's pure Heinz.
When she farts
we evacuate the room.
She really knows how to live.
Her socks prove it.

PATRICIA POGSON

In groups, compare the girl in this poem with the 'Dreamy Girl'.
They have very different characters: do they have anything in
common? Pick out the words and phrases that best describe the
girls' characters.

Housewife

I don't think I'd make a good housewife
Not very domestic am I
With my beautiful face
And my elegant grace
You men must be wondering why.

In spite of my breath-taking beauty
And my deep-thinking, brilliant mind
You'll just have to wait
For some Betty or Kate
That's more the sweet, home-loving kind.

In spite of the beauty of my dark brown eyes
And my cascades of long auburn hair,
Although I'm good looking,
I'm lousy at cooking,
So you'll just have to stand, starve and stare.

It will be a strain on your mind to be married
To someone as lovely as me
But I really do hope
You'll be able to cope
When your friends are all green with envy.

And when you go out for a night with the lads
Don't expect me to wait up in bed
I'll either stay in
With a bottle of gin
Or I'll go out and paint the town red!

LORETTA ELAINE DALEY

Is it fair that 'lads' are allowed out for
a night while the women are not?
Imagine that one of the 'lads' writes
a reply to the 'housewife'.
Write this reply now.

A Boy's Head

In it there is a space-ship
and a project
for doing away with piano lessons.

And there is
Noah's ark,
which shall be first.

And there is
an entirely new bird,
an entirely new hare,
an entirely new bumble-bee.

There is a river
that flows upwards.

There is a multiplication table.

There is anti-matter.

And it just cannot be trimmed.

I believe
that only what cannot be trimmed
is a head.
There is much promise
in the circumstance
that so many people have heads.

MIROSLAV HOLUB
(translated by I Milner and G Theiner)

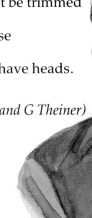

8

A Girl's Head

In it there is a dream
that was started
before she was born,

and there is a globe
with hemispheres
which shall be happy.

There is her own spacecraft,
a chosen dress
and pictures of her friends.

There are shining combs
and a maze of mirrors.

There is a diary
for surprise occasions.

There is a horse springing hooves
across the sky.

There is a sea that
tides and swells
and cannot be mapped.

There is untold hope
in that no equation exactly
fits a head.

KATHERINE GALLAGHER

Write a poem about what goes
on in *your* head!

One Perfect Rose

A single flow'r he sent me, since we met.
  All tenderly his messenger he chose;
Deep-hearted, pure, with scented dew still wet –
  One perfect rose.

I knew the language of the floweret;
  'My fragile leaves,' it said, 'his heart enclose.'
Love long has taken for his amulet
  One perfect rose.

Why is it no one ever sent me yet
  One perfect limousine, do you suppose?
Ah no, it's always just my luck to get
  One perfect rose.

DOROTHY PARKER

2 Memories

Memories

The sound of hooves on stony paths,
The taste of summer air, the pain
Of nettles on bare legs,
The smell of dry hot dust in rain

Bring back the past,
Make me young again.

SARA DUNNE

Memories are often 'triggered' by things we see, hear, taste, smell
or feel. Tastes and smells are particularly good at reminding us of
events from the past. Use an experience of your own in a poem
beginning with one of these phrases.

I saw

I heard

I smelt

I felt

I tasted

The Beach Trail

That was the most tedious journey
ever travelled, the most torturous trail
known to mankind:
at five thirty on a summer evening
with our gritty teeth,
our smelly towels,
with our buckets of rare stones
and shoes full of shells never before seen,
with our ears full of sand,
our skin burning,
our hair decorated with seaweed,
with a piece of glass in our heel,
our mother's radio,
our cousin's beachball,
with an ice cream bar in our stomachs,
a special hunk of driftwood,
an arm, neck and leg full of mosquito bites,
our bathing suits damp and itchy,
with our tempers frayed,

our gym shoes lost,
our money spent,
our holes dug,
our castles wrecked,
our sand battles won,
we paraded down the street
and back to civilisation
as we knew it.

JULIE O'CALLAGHAN

Did you notice something unusual about the punctuation in this poem? It is all one sentence! Julie O'Callaghan's poem is a list of events that happened on a journey. Lists are usually introduced in a sentence with a colon, and that is the case here. Find the point in the poem where the list begins.

Now try your own 'list' poem, perhaps working in pairs writing alternate lines. You could write about:
● walking through the streets of a city
● a bus or train journey
● hunting round the house looking for something you have lost.

13

Aunt Pru

Beloved Aunt Pru
Is never a nuisance.
She always washes up the dishes
Before going to bed.
'Just in case,' she says.
'Just in case something happens.'

One Saturday, she telephoned to say
That she'd had pains in her chest all day,
And would we mind if she died in her sleep?
'I've done the washing-up,
Ironed my Sunday dress,
Put out the dustbin for Monday's collection.
Done the house from top to bottom.
And cancelled the milk.'

We said, 'We're sorry about the pains.'
But that we'd promised ourselves a trip to the seaside,
And it would be a shame not to go,
Especially, as it had been
Such a rotten Summer.

She had to agree.
She always did.
'Perhaps, some other time,' she said,
'When it's more convenient.'

We said we'd let her know.

And that was twenty years ago.

JOHN COLDWELL

When something like this happens, the people involved feel very guilty. If someone dies, this feeling is worse because you are unable to say how sorry you are.

Imagine you have upset someone by being selfish or thoughtless. Write a letter to them to apologise. Remember: a letter of apology shouldn't just try and give excuses!

15

The Race

They were never real eggs. The sun
was hotter then, round on a bright blue sky
like the way I painted it. My knees
wore different scabs all summer.

The winner stood on a beer crate, smirking,
whilst the others sulked. One year, I had a plan
and stole a fresh egg from our kitchen.
It was lighter, sat in the deep spoon safely.

Childhood is running forever for a faraway tape.
I was always last, but that day
sped away from the others, a running commentary
coming from nowhere in my head.

I was still in front when the egg fell,
leaving only sunlight in my spoon. I turned
as Junior 4 rushed past, ran back
and knelt to scoop the yolk up from the grass.

CAROL ANN DUFFY

Carol Ann Duffy says that 'Childhood is running forever for a
faraway tape'. Discuss this in groups. What do you think she
means by this? Read the poem carefully before you decide.

How far back can you remember? Do you find some of these early
memories embarrassing? Why is this? Discuss your earliest
memories in small groups. Now write chapter one of your
autobiography entitled 'Great moments in my past'.

My First Kiss

Our eyes
MET
My heart
POUNDED
My neck
SHIVERED
My hands
SWEATED
My knees
BUCKLED
My senses
TINGLED
My backbone
LOCKED
My body
VIBRATED
My eyes
CLOSED
My head
MOVED FORWARD
My heart
POUNDED
My heart
CRIED OUT

My heart
Sang
Your nose
MET
MY LIPS
IT WAS
MY FIRST KISS

MARTIN GLYNN

Use the shape of this poem to write about your first

SWIM
ROLLER COASTER RIDE
FIGHT.

3 Opinions

Twelve of Each

What I hate's
to itch somewhere I can't reach
stub my big toe running to the beach
taste a mouldy bit in a peach
see a fly drown in bleach
sting my finger when I'm holding a match
miss a howling dolly catch

find a broken-necked baby bird under a nest
have to visit great aunts and be kissed
feel I've lost my finger ends in frost
lead half the way then come in last
touch a cobweb like the face of a ghost
be told off for what I do best

When I like's
to race orange peel down a gutter
rush a tree of jackdaws and watch it scatter
see my room in a glorious clutter
hear a fountain hiss and splatter
a banger start to sputter
tell a fib pat as butter

lick the cold out of an iced lolly
see goldfish swirl under a water lily
draw sand pictures with the tip of my brolly
wrap up snug as a sausage when it's chilly
smell plum pud pronged with holly
be silly when I want to be silly

GEOFFREY HOLLOWAY

Behind. . .

Behind every television screen,
Every gossip magazine,
Behind every cosmetics advertisement,
Every colour supplement,
Behind every television soap opera,
Every home computer,
Behind every plastic pop group,
Every packet of cheap, instant soup,
Behind every cosy little meeting,
Every family circle, eating,
Lies that cruel, real world,
That everyone pretends
isn't really there.

PETER JONES

In groups, discuss what the 'cruel, real world' is. Why does
everyone prefer to pretend it isn't really there?

Poems of solitary delights

What a delight it is
When on the bamboo matting
In my grass-thatched hut,
All on my own,
I make myself at ease.

What a delight it is
When, borrowing
Rare writings from a friend,
I open out
The first sheet.

What a delight it is
When, spreading paper,
I take my brush
And find my hand
Better than I thought.

What a delight it is
When, after a hundred days
Of racking my brains,
That verse that wouldn't come
Suddenly turns out well.

What a delight it is
When, of a morning,
I get up and go out
To find in full bloom a flower
That yesterday was not there.

What a delight it is
When, skimming through the
   pages
Of a book, I discover
A man written of there
Who is just like me.

What a delight it is
When everyone admits
It's a very difficult book,
And I understand it
With no trouble at all.

What a delight it is
When I blow away the ash,
To watch the crimson
Of the glowing fire
And hear the water boil.

What a delight it is
When a guest you cannot stand
Arrives, then says to you
'I'm afraid I can't stay long,'
And soon goes home.

What a delight it is
When I find a good brush,
Steep it hard in water,
Lick it on my tongue
And give it its first try.

TACHIBANA AKEMI

The poems by Tachibana Akemi are about things that delight the poet: Geoffrey Holloway includes 'hates' as well in his poem 'Twelve of Each'.

These poems have a pattern of their own. Use one of the patterns for 'like' and 'hate' poems of your own.

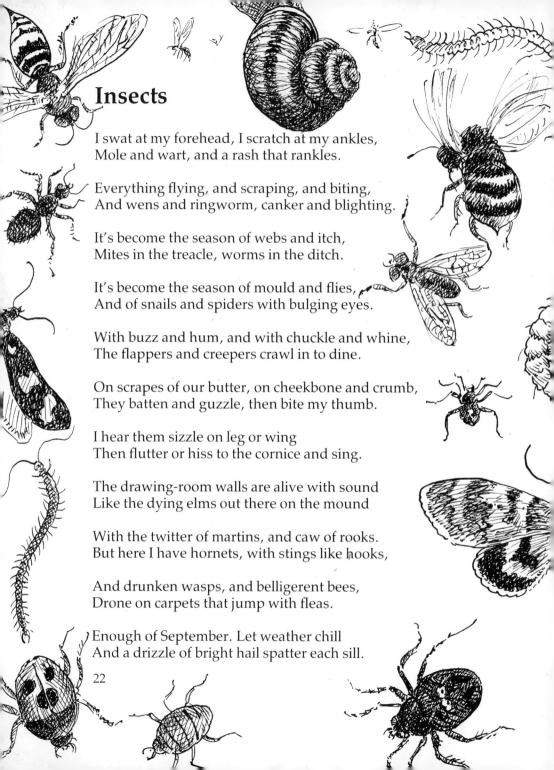

Insects

I swat at my forehead, I scratch at my ankles,
Mole and wart, and a rash that rankles.

Everything flying, and scraping, and biting,
And wens and ringworm, canker and blighting.

It's become the season of webs and itch,
Mites in the treacle, worms in the ditch.

It's become the season of mould and flies,
And of snails and spiders with bulging eyes.

With buzz and hum, and with chuckle and whine,
The flappers and creepers crawl in to dine.

On scrapes of our butter, on cheekbone and crumb,
They batten and guzzle, then bite my thumb.

I hear them sizzle on leg or wing
Then flutter or hiss to the cornice and sing.

The drawing-room walls are alive with sound
Like the dying elms out there on the mound

With the twitter of martins, and caw of rooks.
But here I have hornets, with stings like hooks,

And drunken wasps, and belligerent bees,
Drone on carpets that jump with fleas.

Enough of September. Let weather chill
And a drizzle of bright hail spatter each sill.

22

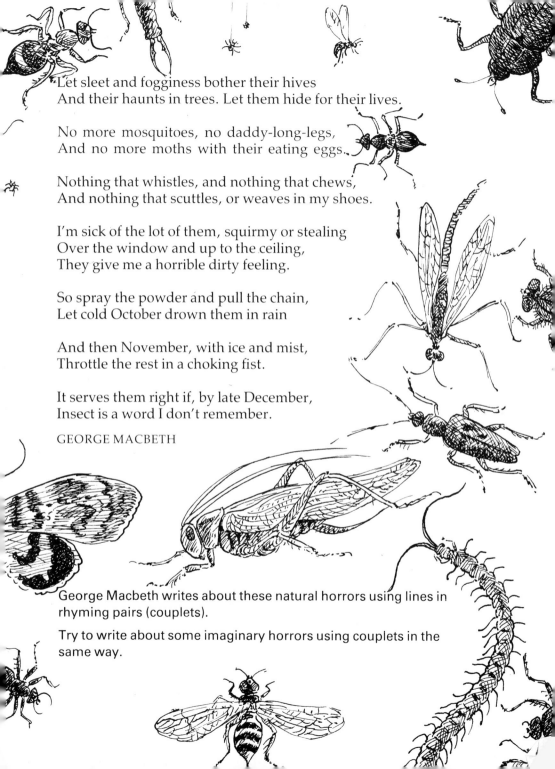

Let sleet and fogginess bother their hives
And their haunts in trees. Let them hide for their lives.

No more mosquitoes, no daddy-long-legs,
And no more moths with their eating eggs.

Nothing that whistles, and nothing that chews,
And nothing that scuttles, or weaves in my shoes.

I'm sick of the lot of them, squirmy or stealing
Over the window and up to the ceiling,
They give me a horrible dirty feeling.

So spray the powder and pull the chain,
Let cold October drown them in rain

And then November, with ice and mist,
Throttle the rest in a choking fist.

It serves them right if, by late December,
Insect is a word I don't remember.

GEORGE MACBETH

George Macbeth writes about these natural horrors using lines in
rhyming pairs (couplets).

Try to write about some imaginary horrors using couplets in the
same way.

To a Cigarette

Friend Judas, kiss me,
stain my fingers brown,
start a malignant growth;
I'll burn you down.
Friends for fifteen years
and I doubt whether
a week has passed
without us being together.

My mouth's foul in the morning,
but you stay in favour
although you've spoilt my sense of smell
and food's losing its flavour.
You're still and all my good friend,
your faint odour thrills me.
It seems I'm always going to love you
even if it kills me.

Friends are often dangerous
even when they're kind.
Girls with skin as fresh as cream
have left disease behind,
and drink, that's made so many nights
so memorably funny,
perforates my liver, drains
my energy and money.

I am in peril on the sea,
I roll my eyes and yelp;
but feel no hatred or surprise
for those too scared to help.
I dream of love, I am hungry;
but I'll accept in the end,
with no diminishing of love,
your empty hands, friend.

JAMES SIMMONS

TEN TALL

Ten tall oaktrees
Standing in a line,
'Warships,' cried King Henry,
Then there were nine.

Nine tall oaktrees
Growing strong and straight,
'Charcoal,' breathed the furnace,
Then there were eight.

Eight tall oaktrees
Reaching towards heaven,
'Sizzle,' spoke the lightning,
Then there were seven.

Seven tall oaktrees,
Branches, leaves and sticks,
'Firewood,' smiled the merchant,
Then there were six.

Six tall oaktrees
Glad to be alive,
'Barrels,' boomed the brewery,
Then there were five.

Five tall oaktrees,
Suddenly a roar,
'Gangway,' screamed the west wind,
Then there were four.

OAKTREES

Four tall oaktrees
Sighing like the sea,
'Floorboards,' beamed the builder,
Then there were three.

Three tall oaktrees
Groaning as trees do,
'Unsafe,' claimed the council,
Then there were two.

Two tall oaktrees
Spreading in the sun,
'Progress,' snarled the by-pass,
Then there was one.

One tall oaktree
Wishing it could run,
'Nuisance,' grumped the farmer,
Then there were none.

No tall oaktrees,
Search the fields in vain,
Only empty skylines
And the cold grey rain.

RICHARD EDWARDS

Point of View

(Heard in a butcher's shop, Bolton, Lancs.)

'It's slaughter – nothing more nor less –
The bombing in this war...
A dreadful thing...you'd never guess
The shocking sights we saw
In London, when the Blitz was on...
A leg hung from a tree;
A body with the top half gone
And nowt below the knee;
A hand with wedding ring and all;
Two feet in socks and boots;
A baby's head stuck to a shawl;
An arm torn by the roots;
While here and there was flesh in lumps
They shovelled into sacks.
It proper left us in the dumps...
Sent shivers down our backs.'

'It's slaughter, sir. I've seen a bit
Of what those swine can do.'
His chopper fell and fiercely split
A sheep's head clean in two.
'It's downright murder to attack
Defenceless folk who can't fight back!'
...And swinging dumbly on a hook,
A dead pig gave him such a look.

R P BRETT

There are three important issues in this group of poems:
    The environment
    Smoking
    Animal rights
When you have read and discussed the poems, chose one of these
topics for a class debate.

4 Experiences

Lineage

My grandmothers were strong.
They followed plows and bent to toil.
They moved through fields sowing seed.
They touched earth and grain grew.
They were full of sturdiness and singing.
My grandmothers were strong.

My grandmothers are full of memories
Smelling of soap and onions and wet clay
With veins rolling roughly over quick hands
They have many clean words to say.
My grandmothers were strong.
Why am I not as they?

MARGARET WALKER

Grandad

There was a hole in the back of grandad's head.
Part of the bone was missing, a flap of loose
Skin half hiding the sniper's handiwork.

Somewhere near Thiepval Wood, trenches
Zig-zagging between the skeletons of trees.

Later, in China, he'd floated
Flat-bottomed gunboats across
The aloof waters of an unnamed river;
Chased blood-drinking pirates through
Shanghai shadows; fired in harbour
Fleets of yawning junks; revealed,
In sacred burial urns, caches of guns
And munitions; watched a man
Hanging
Onto life by his finger-tips,
Above a thousand bamboo blades
Suspended.

And then he had come home again.

My grandmother called him Ted,
And tried to keep him indoors.
Outside, in the orchard, he would sometimes
Let us feel inside his head.
The hole was warm beneath the flap of skin,
Fingers strangely unreal, touching
Only each other where something else should be.

In the orchard, we dug trenches,
Dog-toothed in bays five paces apart.
Sometimes we might fell a tree or two to build
A bridge
Between the past and present. Sometimes we laid

Burmese tiger traps behind the summer house;
Flame-hardened bamboo to the strength of steel
And harder than a woman's heart; sounded
Prayer bells and buried bamboo pills
For passing Chow-dogs to swallow unknowingly;
Filled Mills bombs with a secret mixture
Of flour and water, stolen from the kitchen;
Fed newts to lugubrious goldfish, rolling,
Heavy, in the dank water of the ponds he built.
My grandmother called him Ted,
And tried to keep him indoors.

We played with his man's strength
To recreate a seven storey pagoda.
Bells rattled in its latticed eaves, bats dripped
Out of corners. Occasionally, he
Would laugh out loud, chatter in Romany,
Snatches of dialect that fell apart
As it touched the air. Soon, language wobbled
In his hands, a balloon full of water.
My grandmother called him Ted,
And tried to keep him indoors.

Outside, in the orchard, he played with us all,
And we loved him, sharing the only world
He knew.

Hers was a silent grief: she called him Ted
And tried to keep him indoors.

KEITH SELBY

Keith Selby's poem is about Grandad, but the character of
Grandma is equally strong. Discuss in groups what you learn
about Grandma from the poem, and what you would guess her
character to be.

THE BALLAD OF GERRY KELLY : NEWSAGENT

for Gus Martin

Here's a song for Gerry Kelly.
Listen carefully and see
what's the moral of the story.
It makes no sense to me.

Worked ten hours six days a week,
Sundays closed at three.
They say he made a decent living.
Rather him than me.

Social centre for the neighbours –
not much cash in that –
buying fags or blades or tissues,
waiting on to chat.

Sixty-nine the nightmare started,
Loyalist anger rose:
sweet-shops, butcher shops and pubs
were burned down, forced to close.

32

Who'd believe who never saw it . . .
the broken glass, the noise,
voices shouting, 'Fenian bastard'
–little Ulster boys?

Down the hill of lies and horror
Belfast city slipped.
Twice the Tartan thugs came for him,
robbed and pistol-whipped.

Standing in his shattered shop
and taking inventory
of loss and damage, Gerry Kelly
longed to get away.

Who would buy the ruined business
that he'd worked to build?
No one; so he waited, hoping,
until he was killed.

One dark evening last November –
turn the lights on till we see –
Gerry Kelly still in business,
wife gone back to make the tea.

Sorting out the evening papers
while his son is selling sweets,
in our time, our town, two gunmen
walk in off the streets.

JAMES SIMMONS

In groups, discuss Gerry Kelly and the life he led. Is there a moral
to this story? If so, what is it?

What do you know of the situation in Ulster? What words in the
poem apply specifically to the situation there?

ARMISTICE DAY

As I was going to work that morning
I saw the flag at half mast
And remembered individual death,
A young cousin who choked, a grandfather
Who rattled all night like snoring
And several others.

I did not ask for some time
'Who?'
Being afraid to know
To hear someone's name.

It was Armistice Day
So I was finally told.

Why ever did I say: 'What a relief,
I thought somebody was dead.'
For I remember plural death
As well as singular,
The red mutilated sky over Plymouth
And in the moorland towns
The ambulance men standing by all night
And several other incidents.

PATRICIA BEER

Find out what 'Armistice Day' is, and when the sky over Plymouth
was 'red' and 'mutilated'.

Write a story or poem about your feelings on hearing the sound of
an ambulance in the street.

The Girl on the Landing

Today a girl was crying on the landing –
Loudly, uncontrollably. Her hands
Gripping the banister as though it were the rail of a ship,
She gazed out over the stairwell, eyes focused
On nothing in that house.
                              A week ago
Her boyfried broke it off, said they could still be friends,
Though she knew he was dating someone else. My daughters,
Tired of consoling her, bored with her tagging along,
Had abandoned her, they had boyfriends of their own –
She could hear through the bedroom door the laughter, the
    horseplay.

'Never mind, Julie,' I said, 'one day . . . one day . . .'

But I was one of those who 'don't understand',
'Don't know what it feels like' – one of those
Who understand perfectly, know very well what it feels like –
But have no words, no spell to turn the wind
Or bring her ship in sight of any shore.

ANTHONY WATTS

Why did the poet choose the image of the 'rail of a ship' in the third
line of this poem?

Write the story of Julie's romance leading up to the point where
the poem begins.

Yusman Ali, Charcoal Seller

Some men have lives of sweet and seamless gold.
No dent of dark or harshness mars those men.
Not Yusman Ali though, not that old charcoal man
Whose heart I think has learned to break a hundred times a day.
He rides his cart of embered wood in a long agony.

He grew rice and golden apples years ago.
He made an ordinary living by the long mud shore,
Laughed and drank rum like any other man and planned his
    four sons' glory
His young eyes watched the white herons rise like flags
And the sun brightening on the morning water in his fields.
His life fell and broke like a brown jug on a stone.

In middle age his four sons drowned in one boat up a pleasant
      river,
The wife's heart cracked and Yusman Ali was alone, alone,
      alone.
Madness howled in his head. His green fields died.

He burns the wild wood in his barren yard alone,
Sells the charcoal on the villaged coast and feasts on stars at
      night.
Thinness makes a thousand bones around his scorched heart.
His Moon-scarred skin is sick with boils and warts.
His grey beard stinks with goat-shit, sweat, and coal.
Fire and heated dust have rawed his eyes to redness;
They hit like iron bullets in my guts.
No kindness in him: the long whip smashes on the donkey like
      on iron.
The black and brittle coal has clogged his chest with dirt,
The black fragrance of the coal is killing him.

He is useful still. I shake with pain to see him pass.
He has not lost his hating yet, there's that sweet thing to say,
He farts at the beauty of the raindipped moon.
The smooth men in their livery of success
He curses in his killing heart
And yearns for thorns to tear their ease.
His spit blazes in the sun. An emperor's bracelet shines.

IAN MCDONALD

Disuss this poem in groups. In particular, you will need to think
about:

- the story of the poem
- the character of Yusman Ali
- the language of the poem.

Look back at the work you did on the poem about Gerry Kelly. We
asked you if that story had a 'moral'. Does this poem have a moral?

A Song in the Front Yard

I've stayed in the front yard all my life.
I want a peek at the back
Where it's rough and untended and hungry weed grows.
A girl gets sick of a rose.

I want to go in the back yard now
And maybe down the alley,
To where the charity children play.
I want a good time today.

They do some wonderful things.
They have some wonderful fun.
My mother sneers, but I say it's fine
How they don't have to go in at quarter to nine.
My mother, she tells me that Johnnie Mae
Will grow up to be a bad woman.
That George'll be taken to Jail soon or late
(On account of last winter he sold our back gate).

But I say it's fine. Honest, I do.
And I'd like to be a bad woman, too.
And wear the brave stockings of night-black lace
And strut down the streets with paint on my face.

GWENDOLYN BROOKS

This character lives a sheltered, ideal life – 'a bed of roses'. She
wants to experience the rougher, wilder side of life. Do you think
she is wise?

Imagine a time when you took a risk and 'went to the backyard'.
Write about your experiences.

About Poets

Wendy Cope

Wendy Cope writes:
When I visit schools I am often asked questions about why I write what I write. Why, for example, did I decide to write so many humorous poems? Why do I use rhyme so much? My answer is always the same: I don't make decisions about these things – I write whatever I feel like writing at the time. Somehow an idea arrives and I have the impulse to work on it. I begin to get the feeling that a poem exists and that I am trying to find it. Of course, this is completely irrational – the poem doesn't exist until I have created it. I imagine (and other poets have said this too) that a sculptor must feel much the same, chipping away at a block of stone, looking for the shape that's hidden inside it.

The Sergeant's Song

When a felon's not engaged in his employment (His
  employment) –
Or maturing his felonious little plans (Little plans) –
His capacity for innocent enjoyment ('Cent enjoyment) –
Is just as great as any honest man's (Honest man's) –
Our feelings we with difficulty smother ('Culty smother) –
When constabulary duty's to be done (To be done) –
Ah, take one consideration with another (With another) –
A policeman's lot is not a happy one.

When the enterprising burglar's not a-burgling (Not
  a-burgling) –
When the cut-throat isn't occupied in crime ('Pied in crime) –
He loves to hear the little brook a-gurgling (Brook a-gurgling) –
And listen to the merry village chime (Village chime) –
When the coster's finished jumping on his mother (On his
  mother) –
He loves to lie a-basking in the sun (In the sun) –
Ah, take one consideration with another (With another) –
A policeman's lot is not a happy one.

W S GILBERT

A Policeman's Lot

The progress of any writer is marked by those moments
when he manages to outwit his own inner police system.

TED HUGHES

Oh, once I was a policeman young and merry
                            (young and merry),
Controlling crowds and fighting petty crime (petty crime),
But now I work on matters literary (litererry)
And I am growing old before my time ('fore my time).
No, the imagination of a writer (of a writer)
Is not the sort of beat a chap would choose
                            (chap would choose)
And they've assigned me a prolific blighter ('lific blighter) –
I'm patrolling the unconscious of Ted Hughes.

It's not the sort of beat a chap would choose
                            (chap would choose) –
Patrolling the unconscious of Ted Hughes.

All our leave was cancelled in the lambing season
                            (lambing season),
When bitter winter froze the drinking trough
                            (drinking trough),
For our commander stated, with good reason
                            (with good reason),
That that's the kind of thing that starts him off (starts him off).
But anything with four legs causes trouble (causes trouble) –
It's worse than organising several zoos (several zoos),
Not to mention mythic creatures in the rubble (in the rubble),

Patrolling the unconscious of Ted Hughes.

It's worse than organising several zoos (several zoos),
Patrolling the unconscious of Ted Hughes.

Although it's disagreeable and stressful (bull and stressful)
Attempting to avert poetic thought ('etic thought),
I could boast of times when I have been successful
                                    (been successful)
And conspiring compound epithets were caught
                                    ('thets were caught).
But the poetry statistics in this sector (in this sector)
Are enough to make a copper turn to booze (turn to booze)
And I do not think I'll make it to inspector (to inspector)
Patrolling the unconscious of Ted Hughes.

It's enough to make a copper turn to booze (turn to booze) –
Patrolling the unconscious of Ted Hughes.

after W S Gilbert

WENDY COPE

Wendy Cope writes:

I began work on 'A Policeman's Lot' almost as soon as I had come across the sentence that's printed under the title. What Ted Hughes says there is, in my view, both true and helpful. In fact, it helped me to write my poem. I began to picture a member of the Ted Hughes police force grumbling about his job, and, instead of dismissing it as silly, I managed to get it past the Wendy Cope police force. The first draft of this poem was in free verse – it didn't rhyme or conform to a strict metric pattern. Then, fortunately, I went to a performance of 'The Pirates of Penzance' by Gilbert and Sullivan. My father loved their comic operas, so I got to know them at an early age and I think Gilbert's humour has influenced me quite a bit. (Gilbert wrote the words and Sullivan wrote the music.)

As soon as the sergeant began to sing his song, I knew what to do with my poem. It was tremendous fun to write – I must admit that I was laughing at my own jokes all the time I worked on it. Writing poetry has to be enjoyable – if it's boring for the poet, it's going to be even more boring for the reader.

Choose either 'The Sergeant's Song' or 'A Policeman's Lot' for a performance. The words in brackets should be read by a 'chorus'.

Try to listen to a recording of 'The Sergeant's Song' from 'The Pirates of Penzance' and some of the other well-known Gilbert and Sullivan songs such as 'The Major General's Song'.

Tich Miller

Tich Miller wore glasses
with elastoplast-pink frames
and had one foot three sizes larger than the other.

When they picked teams for outdoor games
she and I were always the last two
left standing by the wire-mesh fence.

We avoided one another's eyes,
stooping, perhaps, to re-tie a shoelace,
or affecting interest in the flight

of some fortunate bird, and pretended
not to hear the urgent conference:
'Have Tubby!' 'No, no, have Tich!'

Usually they chose me, the lesser dud,
and she lolloped, unselected,
to the back of the other team.

At eleven we went to different schools.
In time I learned to get my own back,
sneering at hockey-players who couldn't spell.

Tich died when she was twelve.

WENDY COPE

Wendy Cope writes:
*'Tich Miller' is a sad poem, and working on this gave me a
different kind of satisfaction. One day I found myself thinking
about this former schoolfriend (whose name I have changed)
and feeling that I wanted to write a poem about her. It turned
out to be a poem with a message — more than one message, I
think — but I didn't plan it that way. You will notice that this
one doesn't rhyme.*

Wendy Cope tells us that 'Tich Miller' has as least one message for readers. In groups, discuss what that message is. Do you think that the message would change if the poem *did* rhyme?

White in the moon the long road lies,
  The moon stands blank above;
White in the moon the long road lies
  That leads me from my love.

Still hangs the hedge without a gust,
  Still, still the shadows stay:
My feet upon the moonlit dust
  Pursue the ceaseless way.

The world is round, so travellers tell,
  And straight though reach the track,
Trudge on, trudge on, 'twill all be well,
  The way will guide one back.

But ere the circle homeward hies
  Far, far must it remove:
White in the moon the long road lies
  That leads me from my love.

A E HOUSMAN

46

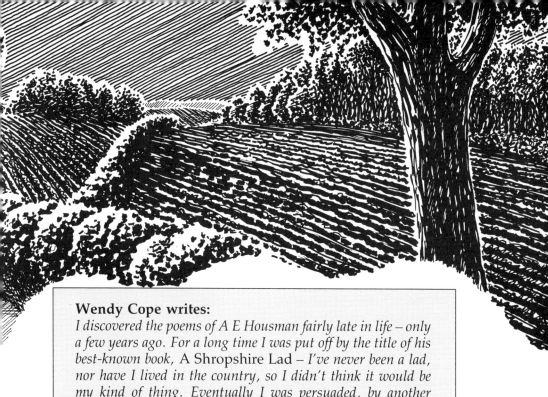

Wendy Cope writes:

I discovered the poems of A E Housman fairly late in life – only a few years ago. For a long time I was put off by the title of his best-known book, A Shropshire Lad – I've never been a lad, nor have I lived in the country, so I didn't think it would be my kind of thing. Eventually I was persuaded, by another poet, that I really should read Housman. Nowadays, he is one of my favourite poets. I find many of his poems so moving that I can't read them aloud without crying. I'm not alone in this. A friend of mine recites Housman to his baby daughter: 'She stops crying,' he says, 'and I start.'

'White in the moon' is one of many Housman poems about lost or unrequited love. Part of its appeal is the beautiful picture the poet evokes with the first eight lines. The music of this poem also gives pleasure – every word sounds just right. Notice the very effective use of repetition – two whole lines are repeated and one word is used three times in the second stanza.

Find out about the life and poetry of A E Housman. Your school might have copies of some of his poems; look for 'Epitaph on an Army of Mercenaries', 'Eight O'clock' and 'Loveliest of Trees'. Copy out the poem you like the best.

Reading Scheme

Here is Peter. Here is Jane. They like fun.
Jane has a big doll. Peter has a ball.
Look, Jane, look! Look at the dog! See him run!

Here is Mummy. She has baked a bun.
Here is the milkman. He has come to call.
Here is Peter. Here is Jane. They like fun.

Go Peter! Go Jane! Come, milkman, come!
The milkman likes Mummy. She likes them all.
Look, Jane, look! Look at the dog! See him run!

Here are the curtains. They shut out the sun.
Let us peep! On tiptoe Jane! You are small!
Here is Peter. Here is Jane. They like fun.

I hear a car, Jane. The milkman looks glum.
Here is Daddy in his car. Daddy is tall.
Look, Jane, look! Look at the dog! See him run!

Daddy looks very cross. Has he a gun?
Up milkman! Up milkman! Over the wall!
Here is Peter. Here is Jane. They like fun.
Look, Jane, look! Look at the dog! See him run!

WENDY COPE

Wendy Cope writes:

'Reading Scheme' was written while I was a primary school teacher. It was inspired by the Ladybird Reading Scheme, which, like Janet and John and several other old reading schemes, is written in a peculiar, over-correct language that no real person actually speaks. For example, nobody in these books ever says 'I've got something' – it's always 'I have the ball, Daddy'. I thought it would be fun to write a poem in this language, using the characters Peter and Jane, but making the plot a bit more adult. The form I used here is a traditional one called a villanelle.

Let me not to the marriage of true minds
  Admit impediments. Love is not love
Which alters when it alteration finds,
Or bends with the remover to remove:
O, no! it is an ever-fixed mark,
That looks on tempests and is never shaken;
It is the star to every wandering bark,
Whose worth's unknown, although his height be taken.
Love's not Time's fool, though rosy lips and cheeks
Within his bending sickle's compass come;
Love alters not with his brief hours and weeks,
But bears it out even to the edge of doom.
  If this be error and upon me proved,
  I never writ, nor no man ever loved.

WILLIAM SHAKESPEARE

From Strugnell's Sonnets

Let me not to the marriage of true swine
  Admit impediments. With his big car
He's won your heart, and you have punctured mine.
I have no spare; henceforth I'll bear the scar.
Since women are not worth the booze you buy them,
I dedicate myself to Higher Things.
If men deride and sneer, I shall defy them
And soar above Tulse Hill on poet's wings –
A brother to the thrush in Brockwell Park,
Whose song, though sometimes drowned by rock guitars,
Outlives their din. One day I'll make my mark,
Although I'm not from Ulster or from Mars,
And when I'm published in some classy mag
You'll rue the day you scarpered in his Jag.

50

Wendy Cope writes:

A lot of tedious nonsense is written about poetry. When I've been reading some of it, and feel the need to remind myself what poetry really is, I go back to Shakespeare's sonnets, which have been important to me for a long time. This is one of the most famous. It says what most of us want to believe about love, culminating in the glorious certainty of the final two lines.

Jason Strugnell, author of the sonnet 'Let me not to the marriage of true swine', is a poet I invented. He is a pretty unpleasant character, who likes to think of himself as a neglected poetic genius. He has written several more sonnets and some other poems too. At one time, his work seemed to be in more demand than mine, and I became quite envious. Why did I invent Strugnell? Well, one day I had this idea and my inner police system tried to tell me it was silly but I felt like working on it anyway... As I said at the beginning, the answer is always the same.

Strugnell borrows the first lines of his sonnets from Shakespeare, usually altering them a little bit. In the remaining 13 lines, he writes about his own preoccupations in his own way. People sometimes refer to Strugnell's sonnets as parodies of Shakespeare but they are wrong to do so. A parody, according to the Shorter Oxford Dictionary, *is a 'composition in which an author's characteristics are humorously imitated'. I have written quite a few parodies, but none of them is included in this book.*

Attempt a dictionary definition of 'sonnet' but this time work in groups.

Shakespeare and Jason Strugnell seem to have very different ideas about love. Without spending time puzzling over difficult lines, decide in groups what that point of view is.

The Triolet

The only form he never used –
That master of poetics, Auden –
perhaps it left him unamused,
the only form he never used,
one that has often been accused
as slight, like Byron, great George Gordon
(the only form he never used?).
That master of poetics, Auden!

GAVIN EWART

Valentine

My heart has made its mind up
And I'm afraid it's you.
Whatever you've got lined up,
My heart has made its mind up
And if you can't be signed up
This year, next year will do.
My heart has made its mind up
And I'm afraid it's you.

WENDY COPE

Wendy Cope writes:

Until I came across Gavin Ewart's poem – a triolet about the triolet – I had never heard of the form. I liked it so much that I immediately wrote a triolet of my own (not 'Valentine' – that came later).

The triolet is French in origin and has two refrain (repeated) lines. I like forms with refrains – often it is the refrain that comes to me first. Once I had thought of the first line of this poem, I enjoyed the challenge of finding rhymes for 'mind up'.

If you are interested in experimenting with traditional forms, this is a good one to begin with.

You will meet triolets again later in the book. Look carefully at the two poems here and write a dictionary definition for 'triolet' before attempting to write your own. You will find a poem by W H Auden on page 78.

Rondeau Redoublé

There are so many kinds of awful men –
One can't avoid them all. She often said
She'd never make the same mistake again;
She always made a new mistake instead.

The chinless type who made her feel ill-bred;
The practised charmer, less than charming when
He talked about the wife and kids and fled –
There are so many kinds of awful men.

The half-crazed hippy, deeply into Zen,
Whose cryptic homilies she came to dread;
The fervent youth who worshipped Tony Benn –
'One can't avoid them all,' she often said.

The ageing banker, rich and overfed,
Who held forth on the dollar and the yen –
Though there were many more mistakes ahead,
She'd never make the same mistake again.

The budding poet, scribbling in his den
Odes not to her but to his pussy, Fred;
The drunk who fell asleep at nine or ten –
She always made a new mistake instead.

And so the gambler was at least unwed
And didn't preach or sneer or wield a pen
Or hoard his wealth or take the Scotch to bed.
She'd lived and learned and lived and learned but then
There are so many kinds.

WENDY COPE

Wendy Cope writes:

A rondeau redoublé is yet another old French form, quite a tricky one because there are only two rhymes all the way through. You will see that each of the lines in the first stanza reappears later in the poem – the first line at the end of the second stanza, and so on. The first half of the first line has to be repeated at the end of the poem. Don't ask me how or why these rules were made. For some reason I get a lot of pleasure from struggling away until I have written a poem that keeps them all. It's a bit like doing a crossword puzzle – you can't stop until you've completed it.

The men in 'Rondeau Redoublé' are mostly invented – I wouldn't want anyone to think that all those things had actually happened to me – but the first stanza does sum up how I sometimes feel about my love-life. Quite a few of my poems about men are hostile but I also write a fair number of love poems (see 'Valentine' – page 52) addressed to one man or another. Like most women, I have mixed feelings about the opposite sex.

Nothing

I take a jewel from a junk-shop tray
And wish I had a love to buy it for.
Nothing I choose will make you turn my way.
Nothing I give will make you love me more.

I know I've embarrassed you too long
And I'm ashamed to linger at your door.
Whatever I embark on will be wrong.
Nothing I do will make you love me more.

I cannot work. I cannot read or write.
How can I frame a letter to implore.
Eloquence is a lie. The truth is trite.
Nothing I say will make you love me more.

So I replace the jewel in the tray
And laughingly pretend I'm far too poor.
Nothing I give, nothing I do or say,
Nothing I am will make you love me more.

JAMES FENTON

Wendy Cope writes:
Like Gavin Ewart's 'The Triolet' (page 52), this poem first appeared in The Times Literary Supplement. *When I read it there, I said to myself, 'How wonderful! I didn't think we were allowed to write like that.' Simple, straightforward and very musical, the poem seemed quite different from the kind of thing that other poets of our generation were publishing. When I learned that some of James Fenton's male literary cronies were a bit sniffy about it, I liked it even more. Poets are often*

> *inhibited by unwritten rules, dictated by the fashion of the times. Now and again we come across something that helps to liberate us from them. Shortly after the publication of 'Nothing', I began to write rhyming love poems that were much more open and direct than the stuff I'd been producing before.*

These poems are not really typical 'love poems'. What is a typical love story? Why do people like them? Is it true that love stories only appeal to female readers? If this is true, why is it so?

Huff

I am in a tremendous huff –
Really, really bad.
It isn't any ordinary huff –
It's one of the best I've had.

I plan to keep it up for a month
Or maybe for a year
And you needn't think you can make me smile
Or talk to you. No fear.

I can do without you and her and them –
Too late to make amends.
I'll think deep thoughts on my own for a while
Then find some better friends.

And they'll be wise and kind and good
And bright enough to see
That they should behave with proper respect
Towards somebody like me.

I do like being in a huff –
Cold fury is so heady.
I've been like this for half an hour
And it's cheered me up already.

Perhaps I'll give them another chance,
Now I'm feeling stronger
But they'd better watch out – my next big huff
Could last much, much, much longer.

WENDY COPE

Wendy Cope writes:

'Huff' is a straightforward personal poem, describing how I was feeling at the time. The mood is a childish one and the poem is, therefore, suitable for children. But, since most adults are childish now and again, I like to think it is also suitable for grown-ups.

Write your own poem beginning 'I'm in a tremendous...'.
Possible endings for your first line might be

rage
panic
mood.

The Sandy Yard

One day at noon I crossed
A sandy yard planted with citrus trees
Behind a small hotel. I walked slowly in the sun
With feet in the hot sand which the leaf-cutting ants
Crossed too, under their little sails of green, filing
Intent; and I thought, this
I will keep, I will register with time: I am here;
And always, shall have been here – that is the wonder –
Never, now, not have been here; for now I am here,
Crossing the sandy yard
Between the citrus trees, behind the small hotel.

E J SCOVELL

Wendy Cope writes:

Do you recognise the experience this poem describes? I did, as soon as I read it, though for me it wasn't in a sandy yard but in other places where I suddenly thought, 'How odd that I should be here, in this particular place, at this particular time. And how odd that this moment on this particular street corner or this spot on the river bank will now be part of my life for ever.' At such times, my mind takes a photograph – I know I'll remember the place and the moment. I'd never spoken or written about this. Until I read E J Scovell's poem, I had no idea whether or not similar thoughts went through other people's minds. We spend our lives inside one body, looking out through one pair of eyes. What is it like being somebody else? When a poet writes about his or her inner life as well as this, we learn things we couldn't otherwise know.

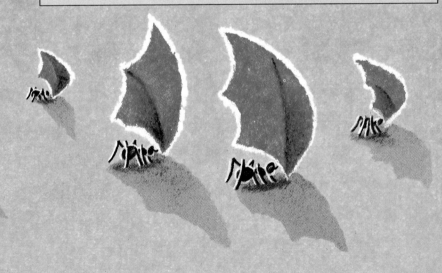

What places do you remember 'like a photo'? Write a description of your special place. Your writing can be poetry or prose.

Love Song

My own dear love, he is strong and bold
  And he cares not what comes after.
His words ring sweet as a chime of gold,
  And his eyes are lit with laughter.
He is jubilant as a flag unfurled –
  Oh, a girl, she'd not forget him.
My own dear love, he is all my world –
  And I wish I'd never met him.

My love, he's mad, and my love, he's fleet,
  And a wild young wood-thing bore him!
The ways are fair to his roaming feet,
  And the skies are sunlit for him.
As sharply sweet to my heart he seems
  As the fragrance of acacia.
My own dear love, he is all my dreams –
  And I wish he were in Asia.

My love runs by like a day in June,
  And he makes no friends of sorrows.
He'll tread his galloping rigadoon
  In the pathway of the morrows.
He'll live his days where the sunbeams start,
  Nor could storm or wind uproot him.
My own dear love, he is all my heart –
  And I wish somebody'd shoot him.

DOROTHY PARKER

Wendy Cope writes:
This American humorist was famous for her journalism and short stories, as well as for her poems. 'Love Song' is a favourite of mine because of the amusing way it expresses ambivalence – or mixed feelings – about a man.

The Life that tied too tight escapes
Will ever after turn
With a prudential look behind
And spectres of the Rein –
The Horse that scents the living Grass
And sees the Pastures smile,
Will be retaken with a shot
If he is caught at all –

EMILY DICKINSON

Wendy Cope writes:
This American has been one of my favourite poets for many years. It's probably difficult to detect her influence in my poems but I think she has influenced me, if only by being so wonderful that she helped to keep me interested in poetry.

If you find the first half of this poem difficult to understand, read on. The second half is easier. Then read the poem again from the beginning. One of the reasons I like it so much is that I had a very strict upbringing. In adult life I have, so far, chosen personal freedom, rather than domestic ties. Emily Dickinson's poem helped me to understand myself better.

Another American poet, W D Snodgrass, has pointed out that many of Emily Dickinson's poems can be sung to the tune 'The Yellow Rose of Texas'. 'The Life that tied too tight . . .' is one of them and, if you know the tune, you might like to try it.

Read the poem, then discuss it in groups. You will find Wendy Cope's comments helpful in understanding the poem.

About Poems

1 Wonderful words

O I have dined on this delicious day,
　 on green-salad treetops wet with beaded
water, tossed by the fork tines of the wind;
devoured the crouton water-birds and
every crumb and crust of the dark-bread earth;
through gristle to the marrowbone of rocks
and the wrinkled grain of high-loaf hills – all
garnished by kindled bush and windrow grass.

O I have bitten into this bright day
　 and drunk from the clean basin of its sky
till only the clouds were left clinging to
my glass and the sun turned on its spit
into grape-press night and finished with
a frosted melon-ball of yellow moon.

RICHARD SNYDER

Pied Beauty

Glory be to God for dappled things –
　　For skies of couple-colour as a brinded cow;
　　　　For rose-moles all in stipple upon trout that swim;
Fresh-firecoal chestnut-falls; finches' wings;
　　Landscape plotted and pieced – fold, fallow, and plough;
　　　　And áll trádes, their gear and tackle and trim.

All things counter, original, spare, strange;
　　Whatever is fickle, freckled (who knows how?)
　　　　With swift, slow; sweet, sour; adazzle, dim;
He fathers-forth whose beauty is past change:
　　　　　　　　　　Praise him.

GERARD MANLEY HOPKINS

Poetry is special in the way it uses language in unusual and surprising ways. In this section you will find poems that:

- use familiar words in strange new ways
- use new or 'made-up' words
- combine words and ideas together in unlikely combinations
- break the normal rules of writing.

Both 'Pied Beauty' and the poem by Richard Snyder rejoice in the excitement of creation, and use a very special language to communicate that excitement. Pick out two or three phrases from each poem that you find specially unusual and discuss them in groups.

Write a poem describing a scene, situation or day that you found particularly exciting. Make your language as interesting and unusual as you can.

'There came a *Wind* like a Bugle'

There came a Wind like a Bugle –
It quivered through the Grass
And a Green Chill upon the Heat
So ominous did pass
We barred the Windows and the Doors
As from an Emerald Ghost –
The Doom's electric Moccasin
That very instant passed –
On a strange Mob of panting Trees
And Fences fled away
And Rivers where the Houses ran
Those looked that lived – that Day –
The Bell within the steeple wild
The flying tidings told –
How much can come
And much can go,
And yet abide the World!

EMILY DICKINSON

Read Emily Dickinson's poem two or three times, then list the
words and phrases that seem puzzling or unusual and discuss
them in groups.

Plan a group performance of the poem. Divide the lines between
members of the group, and decide how the poem should be read
so that the idea of the storm is conveyed to the listeners.

WRITING

and then i saw it
saw it all   all the mess
and blood and evrythink
and mam agenst the kichin dor
the flor all stiky
and the wall all wet
and red an dad besid the kichen draw
i saw it saw it all
an wrot it down an ever word of it is tru

You must take care to write in sentences.
Check your spellings and your paragraphs.
Is this finished? It is rather short.
Perhaps next time you will have more to say.

JAN DEAN

Jan Dean has chosen to write in the language of a child who
obviously has problems with writing and spelling. In the second
half of the poem, she uses the language teachers sometimes use
when writing in exercise books.

Imagine you are the teacher. What would you choose to write on
the child's work?
You may prefer not to write anything at all. What other course of
action could you take?

insu nli gh t

                    o
                    verand
                    o
                    vering

A

                onc
                eup
                ona
                tim

e ne wsp aper

e e cummings

e e cummings is a poet who was particularly noted for using
language in unusual ways; even the way he wrote his name was
unusual! Look through any other anthologies you have in your
school to find other poems by this poet.

After reading the poem beginning 'insu nli gh t', try your own
poem about a piece of discarded rubbish.

Death Came to See Me in *Hot Pink Pants*

Last night, I dreamt
that Death came to see me
in hot-pink pants
and matching waistcoat too.
He was a beautiful black saga boy.
Forcing open the small door of my wooden cage,
he filled my frame of vision
with a broad white smile,
and as he reached for my throat,
the pink sequins of his shoulders
winked at me.

Last night, I dreamt
that Death came to see me in hot-pink pants.
He was a beautiful black saga boy.
And I hit him with a polished staff
of yellow wood,
and he went down.
But as he reached for me once more,
Laughing, laughing that saga boy laugh,
I awoke, holding myself,
unable to breathe.
How beautiful was Death
in hot-pink pants with matching waistcoat too.

HEATHER ROYES

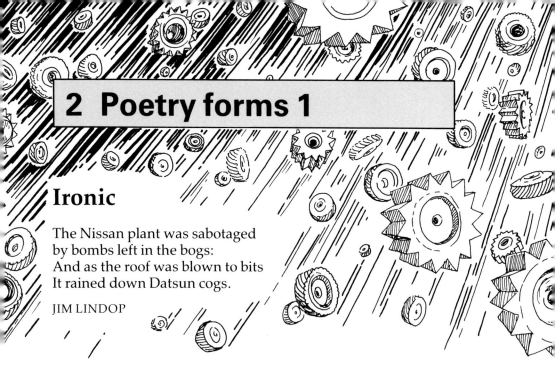

Ironic

The Nissan plant was sabotaged
by bombs left in the bogs:
And as the roof was blown to bits
It rained down Datsun cogs.

JIM LINDOP

A wonderful bird is the pelican,
His mouth can hold more than his belican,
    He can take in his beak
    Enough food for a week –
I'm damned if I know how the helican.

ANON

Gas What

It was six o'clock, the telly was on,
No meal was prepared,
I didn't know where she was.
A stale, frozen pizza
Awaited my belly, then
The key in the lock...
...and she was home.

Well?
Well what?
Well what do you think?

Lovely, darling, super shoes!
No, you fool – you gave me those!

Well?
Well what?
Well what do you think?

Sorry...oh, I see...your hair, it's permed?
Don't muck around – it's been like that
All year!

Well?
Well what?
Well what do you think?

Your nails – you've manicured your nails...
Wrong *again* – are you blind or what?

Well?
Well what?
Well what do you think?

I'm sorry, dear...I give up, what
Is it that you've done?

Nothing!
Can't you see, you fool?

I'm wearing
A flipping
GAS-MASK!!

MIKE GOULD

'Datsun cogs' or 'cats and dogs'?
'belican' or 'belly can?'
'How the helican' or 'how the hell he can'?
'Gas what' or 'Guess what?'

The poets are having a fine time with **puns** (jokes based on words that sound alike).

The three poems are in different forms. Make notes on the forms, looking at:

- the number of lines
- the number of syllables per line
- the rhyme pattern
- the rhythm
- and any repetition.

'Ironic' is in the form of a single stanza from a ballad. Compare it with 'The Grave-digger's Sandwich' in this section (pages 76–7). 'A wonderful bird' is written in a form introduced in *Poetry Street 1*. What is it?

Write your own four-line poem in the form of a ballad stanza. See if you can use puns in your poem.

'Gas What' is mostly dialogue between husband and wife. Now punctuate it to show where the speech marks should go. When you have done this, act out the scene in pairs.

In the same pairs, roleplay and write your dialogue poem: one person contributes one line, and then the other member of the pair gives the answer to it. You will need to think carefully about who the two roleplayed persons are.

Unarmed Combat

Here are
your instructions
for tackling
the enemy
single handed.

One.
First amputate
your left hand.
Two.
As he renders
first aid
hit him with
your right.

JOHN C DESMOND

The form of this poem comes from the idea: INSTRUCTIONS. Find
a title after you have completed this poem:

Here are   Two.
your instructions   . . . .
for. . . .   .
                                  . . . .
. . . .

. . . .   Three.

One.   etc.

The Grave-digger's Sandwich

On Monday I sat on a bench
with sandwiches and tea;
up came a dismal looking bloke
Who sat down next to me.

He was the sort that bored you stiff
The sort you'd like to smother.
'Sandwiches!' he said, and sighed
'I'll never eat another!

'On Wednesday I had bacon ones,
On Thursdays egg and cheese,
But Mondays could be anything,
like jam, or mushy peas.

'I was working late last Monday night,
– there's a lot of flu about,
When a wind came up all cold and damp
And blew me lantern out.

'I'd a foot to go to finish it
The last grave for the night.
I knew I'd got one sandwich left
– I thought I'd have a bite.

'On Wednesday I had bacon ones,
On Thursdays egg and cheese,
But Mondays could be anything,
like jam, or mushy peas.

'I couldn't find me sandwich box
I'd put it down somewhere
I'd got no match to light the lamp
So I felt round here and there . . .

'Found something wood. I thought "Oh good"
And shoved me hand right in,
I was a clot, I'd clean forgot
My sandwich box was tin.

'On Wednesday I had bacon ones,
On Thursdays egg and cheese,
But Mondays could be anything,
like jam, or mushy peas.

'Then as you do, I had a chew
Then dug a little bit;
It didn't taste like much and so
I bit right into it.

'On Wednesday I had bacon ones,
On Thursdays egg and cheese,
But this taste was not anything
like jam or mushy peas.

'And then I found my sandwich box
With my last snack inside,
It was still too dark to quite make out
What else it was I'd tried.'

'Not eating sir?' He said to me,
'Don't chuck them all away!
I'll eat them for you if you like!
So nice to talk! Good day!'

And as I left the park I heard
Him sing from time to time,
Between great mouthfuls of my grub
His little sandwich rhyme.

'On Wednesday I had bacon ones,
On Thursdays egg and cheese,
But Mondays can be anything,
Anything I please.'

DAVID ORME

Ballad

O what is that sound which so thrills the ear
   Down in the valley drumming, drumming?
Only the scarlet soldiers, dear,
    The soldiers coming.

O what is that light I see flashing so clear
   Over the distance brightly, brightly?
Only the sun on their weapons, dear,
    As they step lightly.

O what are they doing with all that gear;
   What are they doing this morning, this morning?
Only the usual manœuvres, dear,
   Or perhaps a warning.

O why have they left the road down there;
   Why are they suddenly wheeling, wheeling?
Perhaps a change in the orders, dear;
    Why are you kneeling?

O haven't they stopped for the doctor's care;
   Haven't they reined their horses, their horses?
Why, they are none of them wounded, dear,
    None of these forces.

O is it the parson they want with white hair;
   Is it the parson, is it, is it?
No, they are passing his gateway, dear,
    Without a visit.

O it must be the farmer who lives so near;
    It must be the farmer so cunning, so cunning?
They have passed the farm already, dear,
        And now they are running.

O where are you going? stay with me here!
    Were the vows you swore me deceiving, deceiving?
No, I promised to love you, dear,
        But I must be leaving.

O it's broken the lock and splintered the door,
    O it's the gate where they're turning, turning;
Their feet are heavy on the floor
        And their eyes are burning.

W H AUDEN

'The Grave-digger's Sandwich' is written in what is called 'ballad
metre' and you have found out what its pattern is at the beginning
of this section. Not all ballads have the same form. Read 'Ballad'
and note down its particular pattern as you did at the beginning of
the section.

'Ballad' is another 'dialogue' poem. What is happening in the
poem? Tell the 'whole story' in an entry in the woman's diary.

3 Poetry forms 2

I shan't forget that funny villain, L,
Who plagued me for a year in Class 4C.
She used to take delight in raising hell.

Her name I won't reveal. It's just as well
To hide the dreadful child's identity.
I shan't forget that funny villain, L.

The fire-alarm went off: she rang the bell
After she locked me in the lavatory.
She used to take delight in raising hell.

The day we went pond-dipping, in she fell!
She couldn't swim, though I could, luckily.
I shan't forget that funny villain, L.

She let the gerbils out: they ran pell-mell.
Miss Pringle ended up in Casualty.
She used to take delight in raising hell.

Although she was a problem, truth to tell,
I missed her when she ran away. You see,
I shan't forget that funny villain, L.
She used to take delight in raising hell.

SUSAN COWLING

'L' is written in a form of poetry called the villanelle. We have
included another villanelle later in this section; which poem is it?
(There is another on page 48.)

'L' is an 'ell' (back to puns) of a pupil, isn't she? And 'L' was a good
letter to choose because so many words rhyme with it. What other
letter could be chosen?

Use your favourite letter for your villanelle beginning, 'I shan't
forget that . . . . . .'.

Dear Diary

21st It's Friday, and mum is gone,
taken by the police in a blue van
with dark windows. She was crying,
she broke the law.

2nd We've had half-term and yesterday,
Thursday, we went to court.
Mum pleaded guilty and the judge
gave her two years in Holloway.

3rd With all my friends gone home,
I'm alone...

4th I am poor. I have no mum.
She was a get-a-way driver,
Dad told me. Dad doesn't cry.

10th Today we visited mum,
sitting in grey on the other side
of thick glass with wire in.

13th   Today, I'm 9.
        I got a card signed
                    'love, Mum'
        but I know Dad wrote it,
        copying her handwriting.

25th   Dad has become a good cook
        and tea times mean favourites
        like sausages with mash and mushy peas,
        or chip sandwiches. Dad laughs now.

27th   We played Wembley
        in the back garden; Dad was Peter Shilton,
        I was Maradona, for Spurs.
        We're going on holiday.

29th   Dad looked silly in his 'Wotcha'
        t-shirt. I looked cool, like Tom Cruz.
        We're going all around Scotland,
        and staying on farms. It's great.

31st   Home tomorrow. It's been really good
        to be away. Sent Mum
        a postcard.

        K QUIGLEY

Triolet for my Mother

I find I grow more like you every day,
Now that I've reached the age I knew you best.
Re-echoing all the things you used to say
I find I grow more like you every day.
Mirrored reflections startle with the way
You walked and stood, even the way you dressed.
I find I grow more like you every day
Now that I've reached the age I knew you best.

PEGGY LOOSEMORE JONES

'Dear Diary' and 'Triolet for my Mother' are both concerned with
the role of mothers. The diary is very simple: ten entries which
show how the child's feelings change, from loss to acceptance.
Look at the entry of the 25th: ordinary things, like cooking, can
become part of poetry. Keep your own diary over a two- or
three-week period. Jot down all the things that mean a lot to you.
When you've done this, reduce the information to three- or four-
line poems per day and write your 'Dear Diary' poem.

Triolets are difficult forms, as Wendy Cope explains on page 53.
Why do you think this poet chose the form for the above poem?
Discuss this in small groups. CLUE: think of the form and look
especially at line three.

Haiku

Black and white hands join,
children of Brixton hold on –
tight, their grip of love.

COLIN NIXON

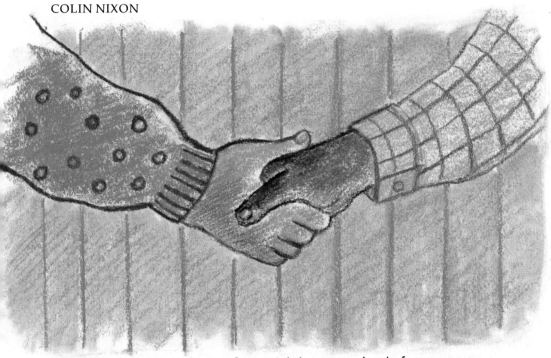

We first met haiku in *Poetry Street 1*. It is a very simple form
of poetry, and usually has three lines of 5, 7 and 5 syllables
respectively, making 17 syllables in total.

Colin Nixon has called his poem 'Haiku' but that doesn't tell us
much except what the form of the poem is. Think of a good title for
the poem. Use the same title to write your own haiku on the
subject.

85

Love Story

He tells of one
    who tells a tale
of love and loss
    of two together
hand in hand
    all he remembers
in the dark
    of two together
in a night that endures forever.

Another time
    another place
beyond the blackness
    light breaks
falls upon
    the upturned face
of him of her
    of two together
in a light that endures forever.

He and she
    she and another
he and another
    what does is matter
who they are
    they are two together
hand in hand
    testifying
to a light that endures forever.

And to one
   who tells a tale
of love and loss
   of two together
hand in hand
   all he remembers
in the dark
   of two together
does it matter
   in the dark that . . .

in the night that . . .

in the light that endures forever.

ANTHONY WATTS

'Dear Diary' was a poem where the the content made the form.
You are, of course, free to make your own forms. For example,
why stick to the haiku 5−7−5 pattern? In 'Love Story' we find a
poet who had created his own form. Look at the pattern carefully.
Is there anything in the poem that reminds you of the others we
have looked at in this section? What is the poet saying about love
stories?

Write your own 'Love Story' in any way you want: as a narrative, a
diary, or in your own form.

SEASCAPE

My son had never seen the sea before.
I chose this perfect, heat stained August day.
He revelled in the treasures of the shore.

He took delight in everything he saw,
and paddled in the ripples of the bay.
My son had never seen the sea before.

He heard a seashell echo water's roar
and sifted sand from spade to bucket, play
he revelled in. The treasures of the shore,

of seaweed, crab and driftwood made a store,
a hoard for home. I told him not to stray.
My son had never seen the sea before.

I should have watched him more carefully made sure.
I should have known that he would creep away.
He revelled in the treasures of the shore.

I knew, before they gave up looking for
my child, the breakers gorged themselves on prey.
My son had never seen the sea before.
He revelled in the treasures of the shore.

ALISON CHISHOLM

'Dear Diary' was about a son (we assume it was not a daughter; why?) losing his mother. 'Seascape' is about a mother (why do we assume this?) losing her son. What form is the poem?

In small groups, compare 'Dear Diary' and 'Seascape'. Say which you prefer and why. What do you learn about mothers and sons? Do you think 'Seascape' is a good title?

Bones on the Amazon

Bones on the Amazon
Brittle in yellow mud
Fires cloud the riverbank
Faces painted with drying blood

Ashes spilt in memorium
Floating face down on slick oil brown
Rich wet cloys the air
Weighs the surface with trailing green
Green into water
Water into wine

The olive vine is a black boa
Curling round the slippery bark
Licking its way to the slime of the river
Sticking like leeches to the grey sediment

The water dreams the dancing
The greedy dream returning
Drumming the returns
Drumming the remains
Beat hell of living daylight
Beat heaven into midnight
The heartbeat is locked tight
The heartbeat is watertight
The heartbeat is whiteheat
The river's on fire

Bones on the Amazon
Dance a green leaf high
The earth is falling through the water
Screeching parrots yellow the sky

We're cool on a river
Sucked in to the winding swamp
Stick insects move in rhythm
Glow worms open their mouths to the night

Crocodiles leave their hearts on the riverbed
Snakes coil their souls to the roots
The water dreams the dancing
The greedy dream returning
Their heartbeat is mean heat
Their heartbeat is whiteheat
Bones on the Amazon
Beating the heat
Bones on the Amazon
Beating the sun
The imprints, the footprints
Stretched skin on ancient drum

VAL BROWN

Val Brown is a performance poet. She is also a member of the
poetry group The Unconscious Collective, who try to share words
and ideas in their poetry. 'Bones on the Amazon' was written when
Mark Williams, another member of the group, gave Val ten words
to use:

bone   dream   dance   return   drum   sky   falling
volcano   shoes   shoreline.

With these ten words Val wrote the 'bones' of the poem in a very
short space of time. She then spent about three weeks working on
the rhythm and form. Write your own poem from these ten words.

Write your own list of ten words on a slip of paper. Distribute the
slips at random around the class for others to work on. Don't
deliberately make their task difficult by making unlikely choices!

The Autograph

I

We stood beneath the punctuating glare
while, through the dark, late June heat breathed aloud.
The actors rushed, self-conscious, through the crowd
in fickle coyness from the public stare.
I stopped him, asked his signature – no more –
and felt the guilt of lengthening his day
of taut emotions in the high-charged play.
He shrugged through tired eyes and muttered, 'Sure'.

He never could have understood how he,
by dint of thoughtfulness, had set the seal
upon my night. It was for me an hour
to treasure deep in secret memory,
and gilded where a moment made me feel
part of one actor's full-spun web of power.

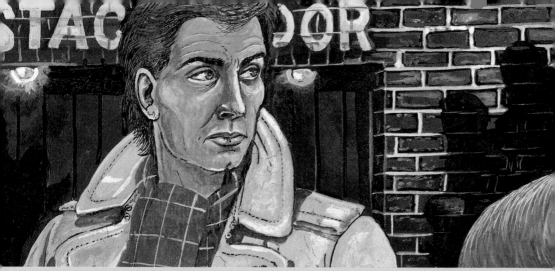

II

The darkness punctuates the moon's cold light.
Four hours of slog and lukewarm, half stewed tea.
Wouldn't you think they'd have the decency
to let us get back home this time of night?
And here they are, all poised like vultures. More
than last night. Same old hanger-on again.
Some bloody woman brandishing a pen.
Why not? I take it from her, mutter, 'Sure'.

I don't suppose that she would understand
the strain of struggling against the stream
of taking home the script just to rehearse
the lines tomorrow's punters will demand.
At least the kid seems pleased. Now home to dream
new magic from the same world-weary verse.

ALISON CHISHOLM

'The Autograph' is written as two paired sonnets. We have already
met sonnets in this book by Shakespeare and Wendy Cope. Work
out what a sonnet form is. Are these sonnets (I and II) exactly the
same pattern as the one by Shakespeare?

Two different views of the same event are given. In pairs or
groups, discuss the two attitudes.

4 Poetry in public

If it wasn't for the 'ouses in between

If you saw my little backyard, 'Wot a pretty spot!' you'd cry –
It's a picture on a sunny summer's day;
Wiv the turnip tops and cabbages wot people doesn't buy
I makes it on a Sunday look all gay.
the neighbours finks I grow 'em and you'd fancy you're in Kent,
Or at Epsom if you gaze into the mews–
It's a wonder as the landlord doesn't want to raise the rent
Because we've got such nobby distant views.

   Oh! It really is a werry pretty garden,
   And Chingford to the eastward could be seen;
   Wiv a ladder and some glasses,
   You could see the 'Ackney Marshes,
   If it wasn't for the 'ouses in between.

We're as countrified as can be wiv a clothes-prop for a tree,
The tubstool makes a rustic little stile.
Every time the blooming clock strikes there's a cuckoo sings to
   me,
And I've painted up 'To Leather Lane a mile'.
Wiv tomartoes and wiv radishes wot 'adn't any sale,
The back-yard looks a puffick mass o' bloom;
And I've made a little beehive wiv some beetles in a pail,
And a pitchfork wiv the handle of a broom.

   Oh! It really is a werry pretty garden,
   An' Rye 'Ouse from the cock-loft could be seen,

Where the chickweed man undresses,
To bathe 'mong the water cresses,
If it wasn't for the 'ouses in between.

Though the gas works isn't wiolets, they improve the rural
    scene—
For mountains they would very nicely pass,
There's the mushrooms in the dust hole with the cowcumbers
    so green—
It only wants a bit of 'ot'ouse glass.
I wears this milk-man's night-shirt, and I sits outside all day,
Like the ploughboy cove what's mizzled o'er the Lea,
And when I goes indoors at night they dunno what to say,
'Cause my language is as yokel as can be.

Oh! It really is a werry pretty garden,
And soap works from the 'ouse tops could be seen;
If I got a rope and pulley,
I'd enjoy the breeze more fully,
If it wasn't for the 'ouses in between.

EDGAR BATEMAN

Poems are often shut away in books; but not the poems in this section!

'If it wasn't for the 'ouses in between' was a popular Cockney song of its day.

Write out the lyrics of one or two modern pop songs. Perform them as poems rather than as songs.

'If it wasn't for the 'ouses in between' had a regular refrain. Can you find a modern song with this feature?

The Green Eye of the Yellow God

There's a one-eyed yellow idol to the north of Khatmandu,
There's a little marble cross below the town;
There's a broken-hearted woman tends the grave of Mad
    Carew,
And the Yellow God forever gazes down.

He was known as 'Mad Carew' by the subs at Khatmandu,
He was hotter than they felt inclined to tell;
But for all his foolish pranks, he was worshipped in the ranks,
And the Colonel's daughter smiled on him as well.

He had loved her all along, with a passion of the strong,
The fact that she loved him was plain to all.
She was nearly twenty-one and arrangements had begun
To celebrate her birthday with a ball.

He wrote to ask what present she would like from Mad Carew;
They met next day as he dismissed a squad;
And jestingly she told him then that nothing else would do
But the green eye of the little Yellow God.

On the night before the dance, Mad Carew seemed in a trance,
And they chaffed him as they puffed at their cigars;
But for once he failed to smile, and he sat alone awhile,
Then went out into the night beneath the stars.

He returned before the dawn, with his shirt and tunic torn,
And a gash across his temple dripping red;
He was patched up right away, and he slept through all the
    day,
And the Colonel's daughter watched beside his bed.

He woke at last and asked if they could send his tunic through;
She brought it, and he thanked her with a nod;
He bade her search the pocket saying, 'That's from Mad
   Carew,'
And she found the little green eye of the god.

She upbraided poor Carew in the way that women do,
Though both her eyes were strangely hot and wet;
But she wouldn't take the stone and Mad Carew was left alone
With the jewel that he'd chanced his life to get.

When the ball was at its height, on that still and tropic night,
She thought of him and hastened to his room;
As she crossed the barrack square she could hear the dreamy
   air
Of a waltz tune softly stealing thro' the gloom.

His door was open wide, with silver moonlight shining
   through,
The place was wet and slipp'ry where she trod;
An ugly knife lay buried in the heart of Mad Carew,
'Twas the 'Vengeance of the Little Yellow God'.

There's a one-eyed yellow idol to the north of Khatmandu,
There's a little marble cross below the town;
There's a broken-hearted woman tends the grave of Mad
   Carew,
And the Yellow God forever gazes down.

J MILTON HAYES

The Pardon Came Too Late

A fair-haired boy in a foreign land
    At sunrise was to die;
In a prison cell he sat alone,
    From his heart there came a sigh,
Deserted from the ranks, they said,
    The reason none could say;
They only knew the orders were
    That he should die next day.
And as the hours glided by,
    A messsenger on wings did fly,
To save this boy from such a fate,
    A pardon, but it came too late!

CHORUS: The volley was fired at sunrise,
           Just after break of day,
           and while the echoes linger'd,
           A soul had pass'd away;
           Into the arms of his Maker,
           And there to hear his fate,
           A tear, a sigh, a sad goodbye!
           The pardon came too late!

And 'round the camp fire burning bright,
    The story then was told;
How his mother on a dying bed,
    Called for her son so bold,
He hastened to obey her wish,
    Was captured on the way;
She never saw her boy so fair,
    He died at break of day.
And when the truth at last was known,
    His innocence at once was shown;
To save from such an unjust fate,
    A pardon sent, but 'twas too late!

CHORUS: The volley was fired at sunrise,
  Just after break of day,
  and while the echoes linger'd,
  A soul had pass'd away;
  Into the arms of his Maker,
  And there to hear his fate,
  A tear, a sigh, a sad goodbye!
  The pardon came too late!

ANON

Poetry recitation was once a popular 'turn' on the music hall stage, and 'The Green Eye of the Yellow God' was one of the most popular. 'The Pardon Came Too Late' is another typically sentimental example.

Prepare a group reading of one of these poems. Make them as dramatic as possible. Record your performance using appropriate sound effects.

Poetry 'broadsheets' were popular during the eighteenth and nineteenth centuries and were sold for a few pence in the streets. The ballads printed on them celebrated events of the day and provided a source of news in the days before radio and television.

Bloomers were invented by Mrs Amelia Jenks Bloomer in 1868. 'Uncle Ned's Description of the Bloomers' (page 100) celebrates their introduction into Britain.

Take a great event that has happened recently, perhaps involving a great achiever in sport, exploration, humanitarianism or politics. Write a broadsheet ballad to celebrate this achievement.

UNCLE NED'S
Description of the Bloomers.

"Do you know Mrs. Pinchmug, I have just been to the corner for a drop of the comfort of life, and there I saw a Bloomer serving behind the bar; she looked quite charming, and I think I shall have a Bloomer dress made for myself."

"Ah, my dear Mrs. Jollymutton, directly I get rid of this cold, I shall be a Bloomer too; I wouldn't be out of the fashion for the world."

COME all you pretty maidens of every degree
That dwells on Britannia's charming ground,
You must be blithe and gay, throw your petticoats away,
Your dandy caps, your bonnets and your gown.
CHORUS.
Away with the petticoats and skirt,
And the gown too that draggles in the dirt,
uigce high and low degree mean bloomers for to be
And be dressed in the breeches, hat and shirt.

You British ladies gay something starts new every day
I think Mrs. Bloomer has proved kind,
The ladies for to please, with the buttons on their knees—
In the trousers you'll look so very fine.

Your dandy shift and stays you must quickly throw away
Your shawl and flounc'd petticoat
So charming you will look in a pair of Blucher boots
And a stunning handsome Bloomer velvet coat.

One old Duchess I declare who lives in Bloomer square
To her housekeeper said we shall be parrots
So handsome and so fine with the breeches tied behind
And a spicy three-cocked hat and a stunning carrot.

Ladies must look out for jobs, be carpenters and snobs,
Tailors and sailors—it's true,
If their husbands them offend they'll give them the ropes end,
And make them whistle yankey-doodle-doo.

They'll think it very hard when they go into the yards,
And into a fever they will get,
Their braces to let down will cause them for to frown,
And I'm fearful their trousers they will wet
Dandy trousers I declare and braces they must wear,
They must toddle down to Moses for a suit.
And every pretty maid, instead of Adelaid's,
Must try and buy a pair of Wellington boots.

To make them look quite prim, their shirts they must tuck in,
They'll be gay and fresh as any mutton.
They will think it quite a bore, for their fingers will be sore.
In practicing their trousers to unbutton.

You must be Bloomers all, throw away the gown and shawl,
The shirt, stays, and petticoat too;
So funny you will look, in a pair of big top-boots
Singing Bloomers gay and cock-a-doodle-doo

The Queen rose in a fright, as she lay in bed one night.
And threw away her bustle, gown, and skirt,
Then she danced in high glee, such a Bloomer I will be,
And slipped on Prince Albert's hat and shirt.

So my ditty for to end, all the women must be men,
And wear a coat instead of dandy shawls,
Be ready day and night if they are wanted for to fight,
And polish off old Nosey's cannon balls.

Ryle & Co., Monmouth Court, Bloomsbury

Let's Rap

Click yer fingers
Ter give the beat
Add some rhythm
Then tap yer feet
Stir in some music
Throw in a rhyme
Blend it together
And it's time
To R
To A
To P
To RAP
To HIP, To HOP
To GROOVE, To CHAT

Wurdz in the air
Enter the brain
There they stay
And they remain
Reach yer mouth
Onto yer tongue
Some are short
Some maybe long
Bounce yer lyrics
Onto yer lips
Move yer shoulders
And move yer hips
Keep it goin
Keep in the groove
Don't stop
Keep on the move

I'm no fool
Coz I'm cool

I'm the HIP-HOP wizard
Like a priceless jewel
I'm expensive
And I'm mysterious
Yer can't fool with my rhymes
Coz they're dangerous
I'm a fighter with my mouth
A verbal politican
A user of wurdz
Superb tactishan
My mouth is the bullet
My pencil is the gun
If I aim it at you
Take cover and run

So remember
Just be cool
To be a HIP-HOP wizard
Observe this rule
Click yer fingers
Ter give the beat
Add some rhythm
Then tap yer feet
Stir in some music
Throw in a rhyme
Blend it together
And it's time
To R
To A
To P
To RAP
To HIP, To HOP
To GROOVE, To CHAT
GET SERIOUS

MARTIN GLYNN

'Performance poets' are currently popular. They perform their poetry in pubs and clubs, even in the street.

Martin Glynn's poem 'Let's Rap' tells us how to perform a rap poem. Martin goes on to talk about performing poetry; like other poems in this section, Martin's poems are part of what he calls the 'oral tradition'.

Martin Glynn writes:
I do not refer to myself as a POET, as the label 'poet' can and does inhibit and exclude a wide cross-section of the community, who, at some stage in their lives have had a bad experience with the promotion and presentation of POETRY.

As a user of WURDZ I feel it is very important to focus attention on any thoughts, ideas and issues, pertinent to myself as a person. Therefore my experiences of being black will figure prominently within the work I write.

Too many times, those of us who refer to ourselves as 'creative people' try to convince others that POETRY must somehow be written, spoken and presented with definitive and concrete guidelines. Although structure, form and shape are important and essential components of poetry, they should be taught as tools to use, and not devices to stifle the creativity you are trying to obtain.

As someone who has done performances, written books, and done things in the media, I have a firm belief in the POWER OF THE ORAL TRADITION, as a valuable part of all levels of communication within society. Even writers who say they write for the page will one day have to communicate to an audience of some sort, which will mean they will have to PERFORM their work. Even the most quiet of readers will gesticulate with their hands, grimace with face muscles, and emphasise different tones within the voice.

Therefore for young people who are thinking about embarking on a career of writing POETRY, I have a list of pointers:

- *Read a lot;*
- *Do not copy others, be original;*
- *Do not be frightened to experiment;*
- *Have confidence and faith in what you write;*
- *Be self-critical, and analytical;*
- *Enjoy what you do;*
- *Do not limit yourself, you can use any medium you choose – music, pictures, drama, etc. – to get your ideas across;*
- *Know who you are aiming your work at.*

Untitled

You are reading this too fast.
Slow down, for this is poetry
and poetry works slowly.
Unless you live with it a while
the spirit will never descend.
It's so easy to quickly cut across the surface
and then claim there was nothing to find.
Touch the poem gently with your eyes
just as you would touch a lover's flesh.
Poetry is an exercise in patience,
you must wait for it to come to you.
The spirit manifests in many guises,
some quiver with beauty,
some vibrate with song.
What is happening?
Slow down, slow down,
take a few deep breaths,
read the poem slowly,
read the lines one at a time,
read the words one by one,
read the spaces between the words,
get sleepy, this is poetry,
relax until your heart
is vulnerable, wide open.

KEN NORRIS

Acknowledgements

We are grateful to the following copyright holders for permission to reproduce poetry:

the author, Patricia Beer for 'Armistice Day'; the author, Susan Bright for 'Eulogy for the Era' first pubd. in IRON magazine © Susan Bright, all rights reserved; the author, Gwendolyn Brooks for 'A Song in the Front Yard' from *The World of Gwendolyn Brooks* (The David Company, Chicago) © 1987 Gwendolyn Brooks; the author, Valerie Brown for her poem 'Bones on the Amazon'; Carcanet Press Ltd for 'The Sandy Yard' by E J Scovell from *Collected Poems*; the author, Alison Chisholm for 'Seascape' in *The Need for Unicorns* (Stride Publications) & 'The Autograph'; the author, John Coldwell for 'Aunt Pru'; the author, Wendy Cope for 'Huff' & 'Valentine'; the author, Sue Cowling for 'L'; the author, John Desmond for 'Unarmed Combat'; Duckworth and Company Ltd for 'One Perfect Rose' & 'Love Song' by Dorothy Parker from *Collected Dorothy Parker*; the author, Carol Ann Duffy for 'The Race'; the author, Gavin Ewart for 'The Triolet'; Faber & Faber Ltd for 'Ballad' from *Collected Poems* by W H Auden & 'A Policeman's Lot', 'Tich Miller', 'Reading Scheme', 'Let me not...', 'Rondeau Redoublé' from *Making Cocoa for Kingsley Amis* by Wendy Cope; the author's agent for 'Nothing' by James Fenton from *The Memory of War* & *Children in Exile Poems 1968–1983* (King Penguin); the author, Katherine Gallagher for 'A Girl's Head' from *Fish-Rings on Water* (Forest Books, London 1989) © 1989 Katherine Gallagher; The Gallery Press for 'To a Cigarette' & 'The Ballad of Gerry Kelly: Newsagent' by James Simmons from *Poems 1956–1986*; the author, Martin Glynn for 'My First Kiss' & 'Let's Rap'; the author, Mike Gould for 'Gas What'; Grafton Books, a division of the Collins Publishing Group for 'insu nli gh t' by e e cummings from *Complete Poems Vol. II*; the author, Geoffrey Holloway for 'Twelve of Each'; the author, Peggy Loosemore Jones for 'Triolet for my Mother'; the author, Peter Jones for 'Behind'; the author, Jim Lindop for 'Ironic' first pubd. in IRON Magazine; the author's agent for 'Insects' from *The Long Darkness* by George MacBeth © George MacBeth 1982; the author, Colin Nixon for 'Haiku' first pubd. in ORE magazine No. 37; the author, Ken Norris for his untitled poem 'You are reading this too fast...' first pubd. in IRON Magazine © 1983 by Ken Norris; Orchard Books for 'The Beach Trail' by Julie O'Callaghan from *Taking My Pen For a Walk* & 'Ten Tall Oak Trees' by Richard Edwards from *A Mouse in My Roof*; the author, David Orme for 'The Grave-digger's Sandwich' & 'Memories' by Sara Dunne; Penguin Books Ltd for 'A Boy's Head' from *Selected Poems* by Miroslav Holub, trans. by Ian Milner & George Theiner (Penguin Books 1967), copyright © Miroslav Holub, 1967, trans. copyright © Penguin Books, 1967 & 'Poems of solitary delights' by Tachibana Akemi from *The Penguin Book of Japanese Verse* trans. by Geoffrey Bownas & Anthony Thwaite (Penguin Books, 1964), trans. copyright © Geoffrey Bownas & Anthony Thwaite, 1964; the author, Patricia Pogson for 'Thirteen'; the author, Kieran Quigley for 'Dear Diary'; the author, Heather Royes for 'Death Came to See Me in Hot Pink Pants'; The Salamander Oasis Trust for 'Point of View' by R P Brett from *Poems of the Second World War: The Oasis Collection* (Dent/Everyman); the author, Keith Selby for 'Grandad'; the author, Anthony Watts for 'The Girl on the Landing' in *Creative Language 2* edited by David Orme & 'Love Story' first pubd. in INVERSE 3 magazine.

We have unfortunately been unable to trace the copyright holders of poems 'Lineage' by Margaret Walker Alexander, 'Housewife' by Loretta Elaine Daly in *Poetry Wales* Volume 19 issue 4, 'Writing' by Jan Dean, 'The Pinball Manifesto' by Allan Kornblum & 'Yusman Ali, Charcoal Seller' by Ian Macdonald and would appreciate any information which would enable us to do so.

We are grateful to the following for permission to reproduce photographs: Heather Angel, page 10; J Applegate, page 39; Martin Glynn, page 103. Commissioned photograph on page 5 by John Birdsall.